ROLE-PLAYING FOR FUN AND PROFIT™

HISTORICAL VILLAGES

JERI FREEDMAN

rosen publishing's
rosen central®
New York

Published in 2016 by The Rosen Publishing Group, Inc.
29 East 21st Street, New York, NY 10010

Library of Congress Cataloging-in-Publication Data

Freedman, Jeri.
  Historical villages / Jeri Freedman. -- First edition.
      pages cm. -- (Role-playing for fun and profit)
  Includes bibliographical references and index.
  ISBN 978-1-4994-3726-3 (library bound) -- ISBN 978-1-4994-3724-9 (pbk.) -- ISBN 978-1-4994-3725-6 (6-pack)
  1. Historic sites--Interpretive programs--United States--Juvenile literature. 2. Historical museums--Interpretive programs--United States--Juvenile literature. 3. Historical reenactments--United States--Juvenile literature. 4. Villages--United States--History--Juvenile literature.
  E159.F73 2016
  791.6'24--dc23

                                                              2015022781

Manufactured in the United States of America

CONTENTS

A man role-plays a cooper, demonstrating the eighteenth-century trade of barrel making for visitors.

Do you want to role-play for a living? Working in a historical village can be fun. It may also allow you to earn money and gain practical skills that will further your professional development and could lead to a career in a number of fields. Historical villages exist throughout North America, so they are accessible to many people. The field of re-creating life in past times, to educate the public, is called living history, and the villages where this takes place are called living history museums. Instead of looking at static exhibits, as in a regular museum, visitors to historical villages—and the employees—get to experience history firsthand. Living history allows one to role-play a character from another era. It provides the opportunity to learn practical skills from bygone times, such as those of a blacksmith or cabinetmaker (a person who makes furniture). The skills gained working in a historical village are useful for careers in both the museum and tourism industries.

Historical villages are enjoyable and educational places to work. They give those who work there the chance to bring another time to life by using historical tools to do traditional everyday activities. When working in a historical village, a person gets to play either an actual historical figure or a historically accurate person of the period. Jobs in historical villages also provide the satisfaction of educating observers, particularly children, about life in a specific time in the past.

This resource will describe the skill sets that are required for particular jobs in historical villages. It will also discuss the professionals in the living history field, such as costume designers and constructors, set builders, makeup artists, and the like. It will explain how the skills and experience gained through working in this field can be applied to a career path, both within the tourism and museum industries and in more general careers such as carpentry and acting.

CHAPTER ONE

LIVING HISTORY

People can learn about life and technology in the past by going to a museum and looking at exhibits of items that were used in that era. However, this doesn't provide a real feel for what it was like to live in another time. Historical villages give visitors the chance to experience life in a past time firsthand. People can immerse themselves in the past. They can visit artisans working in buildings of the period, eat the food, hear the music, and meet historical figures and ordinary people as if they were present

An interpreter role-plays a blacksmith making all types of iron goods.

during that time. This all-encompassing experience provides both education and entertainment for visitors. It gives them a sense of a period that can't be gained by merely viewing artifacts from the past.

What Is a Historical Village?

A historical village is a living history museum set in a particular period, such as the seventeenth or eighteenth century. Employees wear period clothing and perform typical activities of the time to bring history back to life for visitors. Restaurants or food stalls provide visitors with food and drink of that time or food designed to look appropriate to the period. Shops sell traditional crafts designed to look like those of the time. Instead of listening to lectures in classrooms, students can learn history through firsthand reenactments of the American Revolution, for example, or watch craftspeople make artifacts using the tools and techniques from earlier times.

There are a large number of historical villages throughout the United States and Canada. These villages re-create the history and past lifestyles of a particular part of the country. The following is a small selection of historical villages that provides a sense of the various types and time periods. There are many more.

United States

- Claude Moore Colonial Farm at Turkey Run, McLean, Virginia: A small family farm set in 1771.

A costumed woman role-plays a Mexican woman living in the eighteenth-century in El Rancho de las Golondrinas in Santa Fe, New Mexico.

- Colonial Williamsburg, Williamsburg, Virginia: A city set in 1775 with a large variety of buildings and live demonstrations and reenactments.
- Columbia Gold Mining Town, Columbia, California: An 1850s gold rush town in Columbia State Historic Park in California.
- El Rancho de las Golondrinas, Santa Fe, New Mexico: A Spanish village of the 1700s that was a stop on the Camino Real, the road from Mexico City to Santa Fe.
- Hancock Shaker Village, Pittsfield, Massachusetts: A village established by the Shakers, a religious sect, in 1791.
- Missouri Town 1855, Lee's Summit, Missouri: A farming community of the 1800s.
- Mystic Seaport, Mystic, Connecticut: A nineteenth-century

New England seaport village.
- Old Fort Niagara, Youngstown, New York: A fort from the eighteenth century featuring reenactments and historical demonstrations.
- Plimoth Plantation, Plymouth, Massachusetts: A re-creation of the original settlement established by Pilgrims in the 1600s.
- Sturbridge Village, Sturbridge, Massachusetts: A rural New England village of the 1790s.

CANADA

- Doon Heritage Village, Kitchener, Ontario: A historical village that shows what life was like in the Waterloo region of Ontario in 1914.
- Fort George National Historic Site, Niagara-on-the-Lake, Ontario: Headquarters of a division of the British Army during the War of 1812, where interpreters give guided tours, demonstrate period activities, and perform artillery demonstrations.
- Fort William Historical Park, Thunder Bay, Ontario: This site re-creates the days of the North West Company and the period of the Canadian fur traders in 1815.
- Fortress of Louisbourg National Historical Site, Louisbourg, Nova Scotia: A reconstruction of a 1744 French colonial community.
- Lang Pioneer Village, Keene, Ontario: This village re-creates life in rural Ontario between 1825 and 1899.
- Sherbrooke Village, Sherbrooke, Nova Scotia: A village that captures life in Nova Scotia in 1860.

THE LIVING HISTORY INDUSTRY

There are many different types of living history museums. A wide range of "role-players" are hired in the industry. Working in a historical village means performing. As in role-playing games, employees take on the role of another person, in this case someone living in a past time. There are different types of performers in a historical village. People who perform the role of a citizen of the village or historical character of the period are called interpreters. People who re-create an event from the period for visitors, such as a Revolutionary War battle, are called reenactors.

A costumed interpreter tells visitors what it is like to live in the colony of Jamestown, Virginia.

Some interpreters interact with visitors as a member of the village at all times. They act, talk, and work as if they were a blacksmith, potter, housewife, farmer, or soldier living and working in the time period specified. When they answer questions or explain what they are doing, they do so as if they really were that person. This presentation is called first-person interpretation.

Sometimes historical villages also employ people who dress up in period costume and explain historical events or life in the village but without pretending to be living in the past, much like a tour guide. This portrayal is called third-person interpretation. An example is a person who dresses as a colonial doctor and talks to visitors about how Revolutionary War soldiers were treated for their wounds; another is a historical guide who leads a tour through the village. Historical villages also employ people to dress up and serve visitors in bakeries, taverns, shops, and other hospitality venues. People with creative skills are sometimes hired to perform as musicians, jugglers, and dancers in period dress.

INTERPRETING HISTORY

What does an interpreter in a living history museum do? When you arrive for work, the first thing you must do is put on your costume and makeup. Clothing of the past is very different from the comfortable garments people wear much of the time today. Clothing will vary according to the period and class or profession of the person you are portraying. Some clothing can seem very unusual. For example, many upper-class

GAINING HISTORICAL ROLE-PLAYING EXPERIENCE

If you plan to apply for a job at a historical village, you may want to practice your historical role-playing skills. One way to gain some experience in historical role-playing is to join a group in your local community that performs at parades and special events. Many towns have groups such as fife and drum corps, minutemen, frontiersmen, and the like. Members of the group reenact historical events that took place locally or dress up and perform demonstrations on holidays such as the Fourth of July. Sometimes they also visit local elementary schools to help children learn about history. Many museums employ volunteers to assist the regular staff. Experience as a volunteer at a museum can help when you are looking for a job in a historical village because it demonstrates your ability to work in a similar environment.

Another way to hone your skills is to join an organization that reenacts historical events as a hobby, such as the Society for Creative Anachronism or the American Civil War Society. There are reenactment groups for all periods of history. The Living History Reenactment Association (http://www .lhrareenacting.com) does reenactments from periods ranging from ancient Rome to the Vietnam War. The National Society of Sons of the American Revolution performs reenactments of the Revolutionary War period. Members of such groups get together for their own entertainment and reenact historical events or battles. When you join a reenactment group, you must acquire or make suitable clothing and accessories. Other members will provide you with advice on dressing and acting appropriately. This type of role-playing experience can be helpful when seeking a job in a historical village.

women in colonial times wore stays or corsets. Many upper-class colonial men wore knee breeches, hose, and shoes with large buckles. Upper-class eighteenth-century men and women often wore wigs. If you are playing a historical person or a character such as a pirate or Native American, you may have to wear makeup. Larger sites, such as Colonial

Middle school students participate in the reenactment of the Battle of Gettysburg as part of the Army of Northern Virginia. Acquiring clothing of the period and applying makeup are essential for reenactment roles.

13

Williamsburg, employ professional makeup artists. At a small facility, performers may apply their own makeup.

Once you are dressed and made up, you next report to your assigned location or building. There you carry out the work you would do if you were an actual villager. You may do needlework or weaving, cook food, work as an apprentice blacksmith, make pottery, do farm work, be a soldier on patrol, or play one of many other roles. Your job is to explain to visitors who you are and what you are doing. When playing this role, you must speak and act as you would have done during that time period. Visitors, especially tour groups and schoolchildren, may come in groups. They may have questions that you must answer, staying in character. If there is a special event, such as a village mob storming the colonial governor's mansion or a battle, you may be called on to play a particular role in the event. You might be responsible for taking visitors on a tour of a building or telling them a story.

At the end of the day, you remove your makeup, change your clothes, and return to the twenty-first century. The best interpreters do research on the Internet or by reading books or articles so that they have stories and facts to tell visitors that bring their character and the village to life.

CHAPTER TWO

WORKING IN HISTORY

You can improve your chances of getting a job in a historical village by developing your knowledge of history and practical skills. Creative activities you engage in can also give you a leg up when you are applying for a job in the field. Exactly what skills employers in the field are looking for will vary with the specific job they are trying to fill.

JOBS IN HISTORY

There is a very wide range of jobs available in the field for people with very different types of skills. The following are some jobs available at historical villages and their requirements.

ACTOR-INTERPRETER

Actor-interpreters, sometimes just called interpreters, portray real people. They may act in scripted performances or engage with other villagers and guests in improvisational interactions.

They may be assigned to one location or building, or they may move around the village, encountering guests as they go. Their job is to educate guests through entertaining and informative interactions. Interpreters must do research so they can portray their character convincingly and share with visitors stories of life in the village. If they are performing scripted scenes, they will rehearse with other actor-interpreters. Acting training or experience is beneficial. Key skills include the ability to memorize a script and convincingly portray a character. Actor-interpreters must be able to improvise and engage visitors as they are encountered. They must wear historical

A group of actor-interpreters reenact a colonial scene in which a tax collector for England is confronted by a property owner.

clothing and often work outside of traditional work hours, such as in the evening or on weekends. Having a knowledge of the history of the period in which the village is set enhances one's chances of getting a job.

ARTISAN

An artisan works at all aspects of a particular craft. For example, a gristmill artisan operates a gristmill in a colonial settlement, milling grain into flour. This person shares the history of the profession with members of the public. The artisan is also responsible for maintaining and cleaning the equipment used. Other types of artisans are blacksmiths, armorers (makers of armor, the metal coverings that people wore to protect themselves during battle), potters, furniture and musical instrument makers, coopers (barrel makers), and weavers. The products artisans produce are sold in shops in the village. The types of artisans a historical village employs vary with the period of history.

Some artisan jobs are apprenticeship jobs. Apprentices are entry-level technicians who are learning a particular trade on the job. For example, an apprentice blacksmith learns the skills required to make traditional ironwork by hand. Another example is an apprentice harpsichord maker, who makes this traditional musical instrument using traditional carpentry techniques. In a historical village, apprentice craftspeople work in costume in a period workshop in front of the public. The job consists of making objects using the technology of the period. In addition to making the objects, the apprentice must explain the work to visitors. The apprentice also helps research the traditional trade skills.

An apprentice carriage maker is taught how to make coaches by the master carriage maker at Colonial Williamsburg.

Requirements for artisans vary with the task. Some employers require previous training or education in particular skills such as blacksmithing or carpentry. Other jobs require candidates to have only general skills such as experience or vocational-technical (vo-tech) school training in carpentry. For a gristmill artisan, employers may look for some general mechanical or agricultural experience. In some cases, simply the ability to use tools and learn the specific techniques is all that is required, although previous experience is always beneficial. In these types of jobs, specific training will be provided on the job.

Craftspeople are expected to have a general knowledge of their craft, such as embroidery, weaving, or pot making. All artisans are expected to have good people skills. These skills include patience, courtesy, honesty, and the ability to communicate with a wide range of people from different backgrounds. They also need the ability to learn and discuss a range of historical material.

HOSPITALITY AND SALES INTERPRETERS

Often historical villages have food venues such as taverns, bakeries, or food stalls. They also usually have shops that sell traditional crafts, including those made on-site. These food and craft shops employ hospitality and sales interpreters. Hospitality interpreters wear costumes and wait on customers, providing food or drink. Sales interpreters sell goods to visitors, while remaining in character as a period shopkeeper. Experience working in a restaurant, shop, or other service job is useful when applying for these types of positions. Hospitality and sales interpreters must be able to stay in character and work pleasantly with the public, even during busy periods.

AGRICULTURAL JOBS

Some historical villages have farm settings. These villages may hire apprentice farmers. Apprentice farmers perform period farming tasks, such as planting and harvesting crops and caring for animals. Farm-based historical villages may include a variety of animals such as cows, pigs, sheep, and poultry. Responsibilities include caring for the animals while

A farmer in a living history scene at Colonial Williamsburg transports crops in a wagon drawn by oxen. He must hitch the oxen, drive the wagon, and care for the animals.

interpreting the role for the public. Agricultural experience or experience working with animals is desirable when applying for this type of job. Applicants must have the physical strength to do agricultural work.

BEHIND-THE-SCENES JOBS

Historic villages require people who can make costumes, maintain the historical buildings and grounds, do makeup, and create props. Requirements for such jobs are a knowledge of the skills involved such as sewing, gardening, carpentry or woodworking,

LAYING THE GROUNDWORK

If you are interested in a job in a historical village, there are two main areas that you will need to learn about. The first is the content of the experience. You will be living history and describing it to visitors, either directly or through your actions. Therefore, it is important to know about the history of the period. You will find classes in history, government (civics), and social studies useful.

The second area that you will need to know about is communication. You will need to be confident speaking to and performing before the public. Classes in English are important because they will teach you how to use proper grammar to communicate clearly. English literature classes provide insight into the lives of people of earlier eras. If your school offers a public speaking class, taking this can help you become comfortable presenting information to an audience. If it is possible to take a creative writing class, you may find this helps you develop skills you can use to create stories about the character you portray and his or her role in the community. If you are in a vocational program at your school, remember that historical villages employ people with skills in areas such as carpentry, mechanics, and cooking.

Because working in a historical village is a form of performance art, if your school has a group that puts on plays, such as a drama club, you should consider participating in it. The club will enable you to learn valuable acting skills that will help you portray a character convincingly and become comfortable performing before the public. In addition, having some acting experience can be beneficial when you apply for a job.

prop creation, makeup, and the like. Some of these jobs require applicants to pass a proficiency test. For example, working on costumes may require passing a sewing test to demonstrate that you have mastered basic sewing skills. Submitting photographs of items you have created, such as role-playing props or costumes, can be helpful in assuring a potential employer that you have the required skills. Previous experience, such as having worked a summer job at a plant nursery or completed a vocational school course in carpentry or electrical maintenance, can be helpful when applying for these jobs.

A craftswoman creates traditional needlework, explaining to visitors how such needlework is done.

SPECIAL SKILLS

Living history museums hire people with knowledge of crafts such as needlework and pottery, trades such as carpentry and metalwork, animals, and weaponry such as fencing and archery, juggling, music, and other areas. Often students learn these arts or crafts either in school or as a hobby. If you take lessons in a musical instrument, dance, singing, fencing, archery, horseback riding, or arts and crafts such as pottery making or needlework, these skills can be valuable résumé items when you apply for a job in a historical village. Living history museums can help you turn a special interest into a career. Students with an interest in science, technology, engineering, and mathematics (STEM); home economics; and industrial arts/vocational-technical skills can apply their preexisting skills to living history settings. Historical villages often need people with those skills for both interpretation and behind-the-scenes preservation jobs.

BENEFITS OF A LIVING HISTORY JOB

Working at a living history museum can help you gain practical experience that will be useful in a future career. In addition, historical villages offer internship and apprenticeship programs. Such programs allow entry-level craftspeople to broaden and deepen their skill set. Building on basic skills in these areas can allow you to learn skills that can open up additional professional opportunities in particular trades and in historical preservation and museum work.

CHAPTER THREE

BECOMING PART OF HISTORY

How does a person find a job in the living history field? The types of jobs available to young people looking to break into the field vary according to the size and complexity of the historical village. Smaller villages are more likely to have costumed jobs for inexperienced applicants than very large operations. Large, well-known villages, such as Colonial Williamsburg, are more likely to require that applicants have college degrees or previous training for many jobs. That said, larger organizations often have internships for students.

A student intern learns how to make chocolate using traditional techniques and molds.

Many of these internships—in, for instance, historical trades—give students without training a chance to gain experience on the job.

Many historical villages have entry-level jobs, such as being a server in one of the village's restaurants. These types of entry-level jobs in a historical village can provide students with experience in dealing with the public as a costumed employee. This type of experience is invaluable if you later decide to apply for a position as an interpreter.

FINDING A JOB

The first place to look for a job in a historical village is on the website of the village you are interested in. Many of the historical villages maintain a listing of current job openings. Some villages also allow applicants to fill out an application online. Contact the human resources department at the historical village in which you are interested. Talking to a human resources representative by phone or corresponding by e-mail will allow you to find out about available jobs and also internships, volunteer positions, and work/study programs for young people. Some historical villages send representatives to local job fairs.

It is often useful to send a cover letter and résumé to the human resources department at the places where you would like to work. Even if there are no immediate openings, human resources departments often keep résumés on file for future use.

Some museum industry organizations, such as the New England Museum Association, have job listings on their site for positions at their member organizations, including positions for interpreters. They also list internships and volunteer opportunities. Museum Jobs Online (http://www.museumjobsonline.com/MJO) lists jobs for students and professionals in museums and living history sites.

If you find a job listing that interests you, and the village does not have an online application, send a cover letter and résumé. The cover letter should state which job you are interested in and briefly describe how your experience and skills relate to the position. Be sure to include your phone number and e-mail address.

PREPARING A RÉSUMÉ

The résumé is a key tool to convince employers that you have the education and experience to do a job. At the top of the résumé, make sure you give your name, address, and phone number. Next list your objective—the job you are looking for. If you are applying for a specific job in a listing or ad, specify that job. Otherwise, provide a general goal such as an entry-level or apprentice living history position.

List any education or training you have completed, such as courses in history or public speaking or vocational courses in areas such as carpentry, electrical service, or home economics. Also list any relevant areas you've studied outside of school, such as music, dance, acting, sculpting, fencing, target shooting, horseback riding, and the like. If you've done craftwork such as making costumes, props, or sets for school plays, church pageants, or live-action role-playing games, include that information.

Skills such as fencing are in demand in many historical villages because soldiers and gentlemen carried swords.

Next list any previous work experience you have had. If you have worked part-time or during the summer, list each employer and what you did on the job. Include any work you did in a family business such as a shop or restaurant. Also include relevant experience in unpaid positions such as acting in school or community theater productions or participating in parades, historical reenactments, or seasonal events such as Halloween haunted houses. Describe any volunteering you've done at a museum or in summer camp or park programs.

Finally, if you speak any languages other than English, note that.

ROLE-PLAYING HISTORY

Above all, historical role-playing is theater. Just like an actor onstage, historical interpreters must engage their audience, whether one on one or in groups. The interpreter must believably portray a character of the period. Successful historical interpretation requires acting skills. Some of these skills are technical and some are personal. Interpretation requires creativity. You must be able to imagine yourself in the role and time period you portray. You must devise behaviors, attitudes, and stories that result in a convincing performance. Practicing in front of a mirror can help you see if you are behaving in a way that looks natural. You must speak clearly and loudly enough to be heard, in language appropriate to the era. Practicing speaking in character to a friend or relative who can provide feedback can be helpful.

You must be able to research and plan so that you know what you are going to do and say when you are on the job. When preparing for your role, ask yourself how a person of that type and period would behave. You can learn about life in early times from documentaries. Many documentaries on what life was like in various historical eras have been created by museums, public television, and cable TV channels such as Discovery, History, and A&E. These documentaries are available on DVDs or by download.

Part of your planning should include how you will perform for different audiences. Children have a different level of knowledge than adults. They may need more explanation in simpler language. If you are part of a scripted performance, you will have to be able to memorize lines. You will also have to be able to interact with the other actors convincingly. Above all, you must enjoy performing and interacting with an audience.

INTERVIEWING FOR A LIVING HISTORY JOB

If an employer reads your application or résumé and thinks you may be suitable for a job, he or she will invite you to come in for an interview. To make a good impression, be sure to dress neatly and appropriately. Regardless of the type of job you are interviewing for, wear businesslike clothes: slacks and a neat shirt for a boy and nice slacks, dress, or skirt and blouse for a girl. Do not wear jeans and T-shirts, shorts, or old track shoes. Even though you may be working in a costume or behind the scenes in work clothes, the fact that you know how to present yourself professionally is important.

There are two elements that employers will be looking for. The first is specific knowledge. You may be asked what you know about the period of history the living village is set in. For instance, if it is a colonial-era village, you will want to emphasize that you know about that period from classes and reading you've done on your own. If you are interviewing for a job relating to a particular craft or performance art, you will be asked about previous training and experience. If you have examples of work in the area, such as costumes or pottery you've made, you can bring photos.

It is important for a young person applying for a job to appear well groomed, polite, and respectful.

Equally vital, especially for entry-level jobs, are personal skills. Employers want to know about your ability to communicate clearly. You will need to be able to talk to many different types of people, both children and adults. You will also need to use good grammar and appropriate language during the interview.

Employers will want to know why you are interested in working in living history and in a particular trade. Although you have not gone to college yet, if you are interested in pursuing a career in the museum or history field, sharing this information can support your claim to be serious about the field. It is important to show enthusiasm for the job and the field. Because you are young, you may be asked questions about whether you can be counted on to work on weekends, show up reliably, and work hard. It is a good idea to come prepared with examples. Employers are looking for employees who are positive, enthusiastic, willing to learn, and reliable, even when working unsupervised.

CHAPTER FOUR

GROWING IN THE INDUSTRY

If you find the field of living history appealing, you might be interested in pursuing a career in tourism, museum management, or historical preservation. Colleges offer two-year, four-year, and graduate degrees in tourism, museum management, historical preservation, and performance arts.

CAREER PATHS IN LIVING HISTORY

One career path is to stay within the historical village field. Professional positions include carpentry, equipment engineering, and historic preservation. Historical villages employ professionals and managers in a number of major areas, including performers, actors, and interpreters as well as the performance staff manager. They employ historic preservation professionals and a manager of historical preservation, who oversees the employees maintaining the buildings. Professionals and managers are needed for building and grounds maintenance. The director of historic trades employs experts in particular trades. All these

Carpenters work at a colonial historical village. Buildings need to be repaired frequently and new ones added.

positions require college degrees in an appropriate field as well as experience.

There are also administrative jobs related to running a historical village. Historical villages require a full range of business employees and managers. These positions include the finance manager and accountants; the hospitality manager, who oversees the food and beverage services, including the servers, cooks, and chefs; and the information technology employees and managers. There are also a fund-raising manager and assistants, sales and marketing professionals, and project managers who oversee the development of new

TRAVEL AND TOURISM

If you enjoy working in a historical village, you may find a job in tourism interesting. Some jobs in tourism are closely related to interpreter jobs. Many historic and cultural sites employ guides to show visitors around and explain the history of the site. Such sites include monuments, historic houses—such as George Washington's home, Mount Vernon—and historic forts. Guides at some of these sites work in costume. At others, they work in regular clothes. Tour guides also work for tourism companies. These guides escort a group of travelers to various sites and explain the history of each site. They might take travelers on a tour of sites in a single city or in multiple cities. In some cases, they may take travelers to multiple countries. Tour guides must know the history of the various sites they take visitors to.

Tour managers arrange tours, assembling an itinerary for a trip and making the necessary arrangements. Tour managers also must be prepared to deal with any difficulties the tour group encounters during the trip. Tour managers make travel arrangements, oversee guests' lodging and entertainment, manage staff, handle the financial aspects such as budgeting, and do sales and marketing. One of the benefits of a career in tourism is the opportunity to travel and see many parts of the country and sometimes other countries. Often tourism professionals get discounted travel rates. The requirements for travel guides vary according to the site and company. On-site entry-level jobs at small sites may require only a high school diploma and experience such as that gained working in a historical village. Higher-level jobs may require a college degree in travel and tourism.

buildings or programs. The highest-level job is director of the entire historical village.

MUSEUM CAREERS

Another option is a job in a museum that is not a living history museum. There are many museums throughout the United States and Canada that specialize in history. These museums employ guides, curators, and conservators.

Guides explain exhibits to visitors. They may take a group of visitors on a tour or be stationed in one particular exhibit. Like historical villages, museums are visited by guests of all ages. A museum guide must know the history and significance of the collection well enough to answer questions from interested adults. At the same time, he or she must be able to keep a group of schoolchildren interested while they learn.

Curators manage museum collections. In a small museum, one curator may manage the entire museum. A large museum may have multiple curators, each responsible for a particular collection. Curators oversee the acquisition of artifacts for the collection. They are responsible for the arrangement. They must see that the exhibits are properly maintained and safeguarded. They may be asked to arrange special exhibits or special events related to the collection. Curators must have at least a bachelor's degree in museum studies, and in many cases a master's degree is required. Those interested in becoming a curator usually gain experience by working as assistants or research associates for a few years after they graduate.

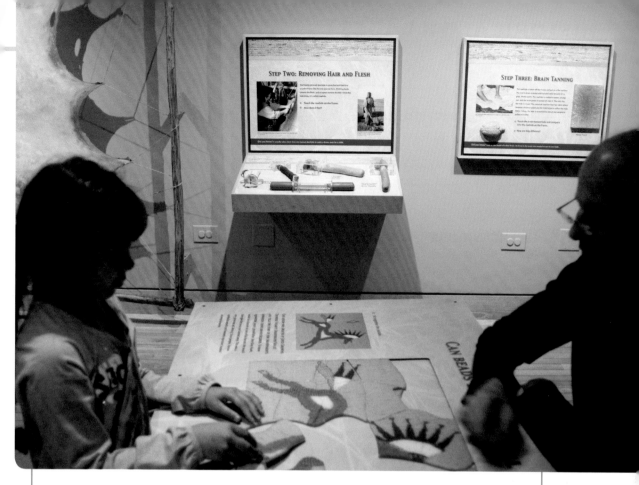

A guide at a museum may conduct special programs for children to help them learn about science, history, art, or culture.

Museums also employ conservators, who are responsible for the historical preservation of artifacts. Conservators assess the condition of artifacts, make a plan for restoring or protecting the artifacts, and carry out the processes necessary to repair damaged artifacts using historically appropriate materials and techniques. Conservators have college degrees in areas such as historic preservation, which concerns the methods of restoring historic items. They gain experience by working as conservator technicians under the guidance of a conservator.

Like historical villages, museums employ financial, administrative, managerial, and information technology professionals.

A large museum may have a director, who is responsible for the overall management of the museum. The director makes major program decisions, supervises managers, and oversees all the aspects of running the museum. Directors of museums usually have many years of experience and an advanced degree in museum science or business management.

MAINSTREAMING YOUR SKILLS

Many of the skills developed in historical village jobs can lead to careers in other fields. Among these are carpentry, gardening, masonry, ironwork, theatrical costuming or dressmaking, millinery, hospitality, and acting.

TRADE CAREERS

Among the trade careers working in a historical village can lead to are carpenter, mason, and electrician. Historical villages hire tradespeople at all levels from apprentice to master. To have a career in a trade, a person must complete coursework and then serve an apprenticeship for a certain number of years. An apprentice is trained by a fully qualified tradesperson, such as a master carpenter. The apprentice graduates to being a journeyman. A journeyman works independently under the direction of a master in the trade. Finally a person becomes a master. You can gain experience toward completing an apprenticeship by working at a historical village. The reverse is also true. Having experience from working in a trade at a historical village can be beneficial when you apply for an educational or apprenticeship program for that trade.

HOSPITALITY CAREERS

Hospitality is the providing of food, beverages, and lodging. There are a vast number of hospitality jobs. They range from waitstaff positions to management of large food service operations at historical villages, theme parks, and other tourist destinations. Someone interested in pursuing a career in cooking may start out as a sous chef, or underchef, in a restaurant kitchen and work his or her way up to chef. Food service managers oversee all operations of restaurants and on-property food services. Hotel managers run the lodging provided for guests at tourism sites, including some large historic sites. Food

A sous chef prepares ingredients and performs other food preparation tasks for the master chef while learning cooking techniques.

service and hotel managers are responsible for hiring and supervising staff, ordering food and supplies, customer service, and managing the finances of the operation. Community colleges and four-year colleges offer two- and four-year degrees in hospitality management as well as specific areas such as food service management and hotel management. Those interested in pursuing culinary careers can take two-year associate's degree programs at community colleges or undertake training at one of the culinary institutes around the country. People pursuing hospitality careers usually start out in junior-level positions and advance to assistant managers before obtaining managerial positions.

ACTING

People who enjoy the performance aspect of working in a historical setting may be interested in the ultimate role-playing career—acting. Acting is a challenging profession because it may take many years of hard work and competition to become successful. Actors work onstage, in television shows and commercials, and in movies. People who are serious about becoming actors need to learn professional acting techniques. Many colleges offer bachelor of arts and graduate degrees in acting.

Working in a historical village can give you the opportunity to see if working in a tourism environment and a particular trade interests you. It can provide you with valuable experience if you decide to pursue a career in a related field.

accessories Items that are worn or carried to complete a costume, such as a hat, gloves, a walking stick, a purse, a fan, and the like.

artillery Mounted guns or cannons.

bygone Past.

cabinetmaker A person who makes furniture.

cooper A person who makes or repairs barrels or kegs.

corset A stiff, laced-up garment that women wore under their clothing in earlier times.

devise Invent or create.

encompassing Surrounding or including.

enhance To improve.

hone To sharpen.

hose Tights or stockings.

immerse To involve oneself deeply in something.

improvisational Made up on the spur of the moment.

proficiency Skill.

preservation Keeping historic or artistic objects in good condition.

reenactor A person who participates in the re-creation of a historical event.

sect A religious group with particular beliefs.

static Not moving or active.

stays A brace, frequently of whalebone, worn by women to shape and make their bodies look slender.

venue Location where an activity occurs.

FOR MORE INFORMATION

American Alliance of Museums (AAM)
1575 Eye Street NW, Suite 400
Washington, DC 20005
(202) 289-1818
Website: http://www.aam-us.org
AAM provides resources, including a magazine, for people
in the museum field.

American Historical Association (AHA)
400 A Street SE
Washington, DC 20003
(202) 544-2422
Website: https://www.historians.org
The AHA maintains an online career center with job resources and information on requirements for historical
careers and mentoring.

Association for Living History, Farm and Agricultural Museums (ALHFAM)
8774 Route 45 NW
North Bloomfield, OH 44450
(440) 685-4410
Website: http://www.alhfam.org
ALHFAM runs conferences, meetings, and regional work-
shops and provides publications and online resources to
meet the needs of paid and volunteer museum staff. Its
website shares information on specific topics and skills
and offers career and job opportunities.

The Canadian Conservation Institute (CCI)
1030 Innes Road
Ottawa, ON K1B 4S7
Canada
(613) 998-3721/in Canada: (866) 998-3721
Website: http://www.cci-icc.gc.ca
The institute offers programs for museum professionals and
students in historical preservation and the conservation
of historic sites.

Canadian Museums Association
280 Metcalfe Street, Suite 400
Ottawa ON K2P 1R7
Canada
(613) 567-0099/(888) 822-2907
Website: http://www.museums.ca
The association provides publications, a online job listing,
and information on internship programs at Canadian
museums and heritage sites for students.

The Colonial Williamsburg Foundation
310 South England Street
Williamsburg, VA 23185
(757) 229-1000
Web site: http://www.history.org/foundation
This organization maintains one of the largest living history museums and offers a variety of jobs and special
programs for students interested in working in the living
history field.

New England Museum Association (NEMA)
22 Mill Street, Suite 409
Arlington, MA 02476
(781) 641-0013
Website: http://www.nemanet.org
This organization provides resources for people working
    indoor and outdoor museums, including online job re-
    sources and publications.

WEBSITES

Due to the changing nature of Internet links, Rosen Publishing has developed an online list of websites related to the
subject of this book. This site is updated regularly. Please
use this link to access the list:

http://www.rosenlinks.com/RPFP/Hist

Bench, Raney. *Interpreting Native American History and Culture at Museums and Historic Sites*. Lanham, MD: Rowman & Littlefield, 2014.

Christen, Carol, and Richard N. Bolles. *What Color Is Your Parachute? For Teens*, 3rd ed. New York, NY: Ten Speed Press, 2015.

Colonial Williamsburg. *Colonial Williamsburg: The Official Guide*. Williamsburg, VA: Colonial Williamsburg Foundation, 2014.

Colonial Williamsburg. *Historic Trades*. Williamsburg, VA: Colonial Williamsburg Foundation, 2014.

Cramer, Michael A. *Medieval Fantasy as Performance: The Society for Creative Anachronism and the Current Middle Ages*. Toronto, ON: The Scarecrow Press, 2010.

Gallas, Kristin L., and James DeWolf Perry. *Interpreting Slavery at Museums and Historic Sites*. Lanham, MD: Rowman & Littlefield, 2014.

McCalman, Iain, and Paul A. Pickering, eds. *Historical Reenactment: From Realism to Affective Turn*. Basingstoke, England: Palgrave Macmillian, 2010.

Melber, Leah M. *Teaching the Museum: Careers in Museum Education*. Washington, DC: American Alliance of Museums, 2014.

Roth, Stacy Flora. *Past into Present: Effective Techniques for First-Person Historical Interpretation*. Chapel Hill, NC: University of North Carolina Press, 1998.

Schneider, Rebecca. *Performing Remains: Art and War in Times of Theatrical Reenactment*. New York, NY: Routledge, 2011.

HISTORICAL VILLAGES

Schroeder, Charlie. *Man of War: My Adventures in the World of Historical Reenactment.* New York, NY: Penguin, 2013.

Simon, Nina. *The Participatory Museum.* Santa Cruz, CA: Museum 2.0, 2010.

Stein, Jeannine. *Battlefields of Honor: American Civil War Reenactors.* London, England, and New York, NY: Merrell, 2012.

Stevens, Greg, and Wendy Luke. *A Life in Museums: Managing Your Museum Career.* Washington, DC: American Alliance of Museums, 2013.

Terry, Andrea. *Family Ties: Living History in Canadian House Museums.* Montreal, QC: McGill-Queens University Press, 2015.

Van Balgooy, Max. *Interpreting African American History and Culture at Museums and Historic Sites.* Lanham, MD: Rowman & Littlefield, 2014.

Walhimer, Mark. *Museums 101.* Lanham, MD: Rowman & Littlefield, 2015.

BIBLIOGRAPHY

American Historical Association. "Careers in Public History." Retrieved April 20, 2015 (https://www.historians.org/jobs-and-professional-development/career-resources/careers-in-public-history).

American Historical Association. "Historians in Museums." Retrieved April 25, 2015 (http://www.historians.org/jobs-and-professional-development/career-resources/careers-for-students-of-history/historians-in-museums #2overview).

American Institute for the Conservation of Historic and Artistic Works. "Careers in Conservation." Retrieved May 10, 2015 (http://www.conservation-us.org/publications-resources/careers-in-conservation/become-a-conservator# .VVf2D7IViko).

Art Project, The. "Oversee Great Collections of Art as a Museum Curator." Retrieved May 10, 2015 (http://www.theartcareerproject.com/gain-creative-control-with-a-museum-curator-career/556).

College Board, The. Career: Curator. Retrieved May 5, 2015 (https://bigfuture .collegeboard.org/careers/education-museum-work-library-science-curators).

Colonial Williamsburg Foundation. "Careers at Colonial Williamsburg." Retrieved February 26, 2015 (http://www.history.org/foundation/careers).

Colonial Williamsburg Foundation. *Colonial Williamsburg*. Williamsburg, VA: Colonial Williamsburg Foundation, 2014.

HCareers. "Career Paths of a Hospitality Management Student." Retrieved May 10, 2015 (http://www.hcareers.com/us/resourcecenter/tabid/306/articleid/573/default.aspx).

Magelssen, Scott. *Living History Museums: Undoing History through Performance*. Lanham, MD: The Scarecrow Press, 2007.

Old Sturbridge Village. *The Outdoor Living History Museum*. Sturbridge, MA: Old Sturbridge Village, 2009.

Pont, Lyn. *Hospitality Management*. Bloomington, IN: Manners Press, 2015.

Smithsonian. "Museum Studies." Retrieved April 14, 2014 (http://museumstudies .si.edu/careers.html).

Wright, Lee. "Getting a Job as an Interpreter at a Historic Site: What to Include on Your Resume and Why." November 12, 2013. Retrieved May 10, 2015 (http://www.thehistorylist.com/blog_posts/getting-a-job-as-an-interpreter-at-a-historic-site-what-to-include-on-your-resume-and-why).

Yoffe, Emily. "A Colonial Dame: My Brief, Inspiring Career as a Historical Re-enactor." *Slate*. Retrieved February 26, 2015 (http://www.slate.com/articles/life/human_guinea_pig/2008/12/a_colonial_dame.html).

INDEX

ABOUT THE AUTHOR

Jeri Freedman has a B.A. degree from Harvard University. She is the author of more than fifty nonfiction children's and young adult books, including *Massachusetts Past and Present*, *Iowa Past and Present*, *Louisiana Past and Present*, *A Primary Source History of Colonial Massachusetts*, and numerous career guides for young people.

PHOTO CREDITS